"BE KIND TO YOUR GUEST!"

Grolier Enterprises Inc. offers a varied selection of both adult and children's book racks. For details on ordering, please write: Grolier Enterprises Inc., Sherman Turnpike, Danbury, CT 06816 Attn: Premium Department

CREDITS

Producer
Ron Berry

Editor
Orly Kelly

Printed in the United States of America.

What to do when your mom or dad says . . .

"BE KIND TO YOUR GUEST!"

By
JOY BERRY

GROLIER ENTERPRISES CORP.

Has your mother or father ever told you to ...

When your parents tell you to be kind to your guest, do you wonder ...

If any of this sounds familiar to you, you're going to **love** this book.

Because this book is going to tell you exactly how to treat guests.

INVITING SOMEONE TO YOUR HOME

This is Randy Rude.

Whenever Randy Rude invites someone to his home, he talks with his parents about it in front of the other person. Sometimes this is embarrassing.

Whenever you invite someone to your home, you can be gracious by doing these things:

1. Before you invite anyone to your home, make sure the visit will not conflict with any of your family's plans.

2. Get permission from your parents to have the person come to your house. It's best if you do not ask them in front of the other person, because it may be embarrassing for everyone if your parents have to say "No."

3. Make sure the other person gets permission from his or her parents to come. Again, it's best that you allow the person to talk with his or her parents privately.

4. **Give the other person all the necessary information regarding the visit – who will be there, what to wear or bring, when to arrive, where you live, etc.**

ANSWERING THE DOOR

Whenever someone is at the door, Randy Rude makes the person wait a long time before he opens it.

Whenever Randy Rude answers the door, he throws it open and greets the visitor abruptly. Randy is not very gracious.

When you greet someone at the door, you can be gracious by doing these things:

1. Open the door gently.

2. Greet the visitor kindly.

3. If the person at the door is someone like the mail carrier, you do not have to invite him or her in (unless the weather is very bad). Instead, accept the delivery, say "Thank you," and bid him or her a good day.

4. If the person at the door is a stranger, politely find out what he or she wants.

REMEMBER — NEVER OPEN THE DOOR FOR A STRANGER IF YOU ARE HOME ALONE!

5. If the person at the door is someone you know, invite him or her in.

6. Once the visitor is inside the house, you will want to —

  - take the visitor's coat if they want you to, and put it in an appropriate place; then

  - offer the visitor a seat.

ANSWERING THE DOOR AND FINDING THAT THE PERSON WANTS TO TALK WITH YOU

If a visitor at the door wishes to speak with Randy Rude, Randy acts as if he is uninterested in anything the person has to say.

Randy also makes the person stand outside during the entire conversation. Randy is not very gracious.

Whenever a visitor at the door wants to talk with you, you can be gracious by doing these things:

1. Invite the visitor in.

2. Take the visitor's coat (if he or she wants you to), and put it in an appropriate place.

3. **Offer the visitor a seat.**

4. **Talk with the visitor.**

It is not necessary for you to follow these four steps —

– if the visitor's message is a short one; or

– if the visitor is uninvited, and you are not able or do not want to talk with him or her.

DEANA, CAN I TALK TO YOU?
OH, I'M SORRY! THIS ISN'T A VERY GOOD TIME, BUT MAYBE WE CAN TALK SOME OTHER TIME!

ANSWERING THE DOOR AND FINDING THAT THE PERSON WANTS TO TALK TO SOMEONE ELSE

If a visitor at the door wishes to talk with someone other than him, Randy becomes annoyed and is often rude.

If the visitor at the door wishes to speak with someone other than Randy, Randy doesn't go to get the person. Instead, he yells for the person. Randy is not very gracious.

Whenever a visitor at the door wants to talk with someone other than you, you can be gracious by doing these things:

1. Politely ask the visitor to wait while you go to get the other person.

2. Go to get the other person and ask them to come to the door.

3. If necessary, take a message. If the other person is not home or cannot come to the door, get the visitor's name, telephone number, and/or message. (You may want to have the visitor write all of this down.)

4. If necessary, deliver the message. Assure the visitor that you will relay his or her message to the other person, and then make sure you do it.

HAVING SOMEONE IN YOUR HOME

When Randy Rude has someone in his home, he often ignores the person. He expects the person to entertain himself or herself.

When Randy Rude isn't neglecting his guests, he is bossing them around. If the other person does not do exactly what Randy wants, Randy tells the person to go home.

Whenever you have someone in your home, you can be gracious by doing these things:

1. Prepare your home before your guest arrives. Make sure it is clean and, if he or she is staying overnight, make sure there is bedding, towels, drawer and closet space, and coat hangers for the person.

2. Plan some things to do together, things you think he or she will enjoy doing.

3. Don't depend on him or her or anyone in your family to entertain you.

4. **If the person does not like the activities you have planned, allow him or her to make suggestions and do your best to cooperate.**

5. **Take care of your guest. Do not leave him or her for long periods of time.**

6. **Eat only when there is enough to share with your guest, and serve your guest first.**

7. **Share as many of your things as you can.**

8. You and your guest should be responsible for cleaning up any mess you make.

9. When your guest is ready to leave, help gather up all of his or her things.

10. Walk with the person to the door and say something like, "I'm glad you could come," as he or she is leaving.

Whenever people come to your home, they will respond to you much better if you treat them the way you would want to be treated. This is the most important thing to remember whenever anyone visits you.

THE END of unhappy guests.